D0497667

A TIME FOR EVERYTHING

EVERYTHING

Discovering the Beautiful Rhythms of Life

MARGARET FEINBERG

FOREWORD BY PATSY CLAIRMONT

THOMAS NELSON
Since 1798

NASHVILLE   MEXICO CITY   RIO DE JANEIRO

© 2013 Thomas Nelson

All rights reserved. No portion of this book may be reproduced, stored in a retrieval system, or transmitted in any form or by any means—electronic, mechanical, photocopy, recording, or any other—except for brief quotations in printed reviews, without the prior permission of the publisher.

Published in Nashville, Tennessee, by Thomas Nelson. Thomas Nelson is a trademark of Thomas Nelson, Inc.

Thomas Nelson, Inc., titles may be purchased in bulk for educational, business, fund-raising, or sales promotional use. For information, please e-mail SpecialMarkets@ThomasNelson.com.

All Scripture quotations are taken from THE NEW KING JAMES VERSION. © 1982 by Thomas Nelson, Inc. Used by permission. All rights reserved.

Page design: Crosslin Creative

978-1-4016-7623-0

Printed in China

15 16 17 DSC 8 7 6

Contents

Foreword

I love watching Spring win over Winter. Take the hyacinth: she butts her pretty little head against the half-frozen earth and somehow wins. Up she comes from the darkness shouting victory in pink, purple, and white regalia. And even when she finds herself petal-deep in late snow she shakes it off and lifts her curly bob to the sun. You can almost hear her sing, "I got rhythm, I got rhythm" because that girl knows how to move to the music of her design. And Hyacinth is aware as she pushes through the hardship of her circumstances that it's her season to bloom. And nothing is going to stop her—not winter's icy grip and not earth's dark tomb.

We hear the Creator's song throughout creation in white-capped waves as they lap the shores, we see it in the drifting art of shifting sands, we listen to it in the soprano performance of a sparrow on a fence post, and in the raucous pattern of luminous raindrops splattering across rooftops. We also experience it in our lives again and again as Spring skips into Summer, and Summer cools into Fall, and Fall snowballs into Winter, and Winter melts back into Spring.

I remember, in the Spring of my life, being a young mother nestling with my infant and feeling the reassuring beat of his heart against my body. There's just something about rhythm that communicates the harmony life was meant to have. Today I am in a very different season as my autumn oh-so-quickly turns to winter-white. Now I watch and applaud my son's children as they lean into the wind to test their wings and write their names in the sky.

This study will help us, regardless of our season, to realign our hearts with the Lord so we too, like our friend Hyacinth, can shake off hardship, gain strength, and get into life-changing rhythms. Balance is such an elusive butterfly, but when we hear Christ's voice and move in that direction the cacophony of our chaotic existence settles down to a comforting lullaby. Oh, no doubt, our circumstances will still swirl, but our thoughts and heartbeat find their quietness and confidence in Christ. For His way is peace and His paths light and grace . . . all notes in His divine song that He sings over us. The Lord has a prescribed plan that will add balance to the relational and emotional landscape of our life.

C'mon girlfriends, the world is full of toe-tapping music placed there by the Creator. Yes, let's pat our hands and even kick up our heels to celebrate the rising of the sun and the setting of the same. Solomon, the writer of Ecclesiastes, puts it this way: "To everything there is a season" (3:1). And in this study we will examine verses for mind-counsel and emotional encouragement. So once you've finished twirling about, settle in—with perhaps a glass of iced sweet tea, or a cup of steamy hot cocoa, depending on your season—and let's listen for the rhythms that keep us in bloom.

—Patsy Clairmont

Introduction

A Season for Everything

But seek first the kingdom of God and His righteousness, and all
these things shall be added to you.

Matthew 6:33

Imagine trying to stay balanced on top of a ball. How long could you
last? A few seconds? A few minutes? Perhaps longer?

As busy women, so many of us want more balance in our lives, but
balance is impossible to maintain. Sometimes life picks up speed without
warning or slows down unexpectedly. Sometimes we're pulled in many
directions all at once. Sometimes we find ourselves pushed by our
schedules, commitments, and unexpected needs in life. And any sense of
balance is lost.

Instead of trying to stay perfectly balanced all the time (an impossible
act!), the Bible challenges us to pay attention to the season of life we're in
and recognize that there's a time for everything. Some seasons of life will
naturally be fast-paced; others will be more relaxed. Some seasons of life
will be marked by transition and change; others will be defined by their
steadiness. Some seasons in life will challenge us to give; others will teach
us to receive. Some seasons of life are marked by new beginnings; others
by necessary endings.

The a-m-a-z-i-n-g news of being a child of God is that no matter what
season of life we find ourselves in we have the opportunity to seek and
celebrate God right in the midst. We can choose to grow in the fullness
of all God has called and created us to be. Becoming more Christlike isn't

something that's just awaiting you in your next season of life—it's available to you right now!

In this study, we're going to look at some of the seasons of life spotlighted in the book of Ecclesiastes. This book of the Bible is a powerful reminder that life is meaningless unless centered upon God. Scholars debate over true authorship of the book, but tradition has attributed the book to King Solomon.

My hope and prayer is that through this study you'll not only recognize the wondrous season God has you in right now but that you'll embrace it as a gift and, in the process, become more Christlike each and every day.

Blessings,
Margaret Feinberg

Right on Time

Have you ever found yourself wondering, "Why did this happen right now?" or "Why did this happen so soon?" or "Why couldn't this have waited to happen?" Sometimes it's easy to forget that God's timing is not our own. Rest assured that God has a time for everything under heaven. And He is with you every step of the way.

To everything there is a season.

Ecclesiastes 3:1

A Time for Everything

Spring and Summer, Winter and Fall

What's your favorite season of the year?

Some people come alive in spring. The scent of flowers blossoming, the sight of lime-green leaves, and the sound of baby birds chirping all tend to remind us of the gift of new life.

Others adore summer. The long days of this season encourage us to get out and about. Summer invites us to become more active and engaged in our neighborhoods and communities, embracing the warmth of the sun, the splash of cool waters, the gentleness of shade on a hot day.

Still others enjoy fall. Cooling temperatures, the crunch of colorful leaves, and the occasional whiff of smoke from a neighbor's chimney are all reminders that change is in the air. The new life that budded in spring has come to a beautiful end. Fall invites us to unpack our snuggly warm clothes and enjoy gathering indoors again.

And still others love winter. The crisp, cool days are short; the colder starry nights are long. This is where the end-of-the-year holidays await. Winter beckons us indoors, often slowing our pace and inviting us to rest.

Though we may have a season that's our favorite, every season offers something different to appreciate and celebrate. Reflecting on the changing of seasons reminds us that everything has its appointed time.

In the book of Ecclesiastes, Solomon echoed this idea when he wrote that an appointed time, an actual season, exists for every activity under the heavens (3:1).

Consider what Solomon observed:

Every season is hand-selected by God for a particular purpose.

[There's] a time to be born,
And a time to die;
A time to plant,
And a time to pluck what is planted;
A time to kill,
And a time to heal;
A time to break down,
And a time to build up;
A time to weep,
And a time to laugh;
A time to mourn,
And a time to dance;
A time to cast away stones,
And a time to gather stones;
A time to embrace,
And a time to refrain from embracing;
A time to gain,
And a time to lose;
A time to keep,
And a time to throw away;
A time to tear,
And a time to sew;
A time to keep silence,

And a time to speak;
A time to love,
And a time to hate;
A time of war,
And a time of peace. (Ecclesiastes 3:2–8)

Though we may have a natural affinity toward one season over another, each and every one is hand-selected by God for a particular purpose. As we learn to accept these times in life as gifts, we find ourselves celebrating the goodness of God no matter what situation we are in.

1. What is your favorite season: spring, summer, fall, or winter? Why?

2. Reflecting on the four seasons, which one best describes your life situation right now?

King Solomon, known for his vast wisdom, wrote a poem in Ecclesiastes that describes God's role in the timing of life's seasons. Ecclesiastes 3:1–8 is best understood as Hebrew poetry and more specifically as a form of parallelism in which the author uses opposites and antonyms to describe and illustrate the author's point. Solomon illustrated that nothing can be done without depending on and acknowledging God.

3. Read **Ecclesiastes 3:1–8** again. In the space below, write down the five times in Solomon's list that you most enjoy. Write down the five least enjoyable times of life that Solomon lists.

Times You Most Enjoy:	Times You Least Enjoy:
1.	1.
2.	2.
3.	3.
4.	4.
5.	5.

We all have seasons in life that we prefer more than others, but each one provides an opportunity to learn something more about God. Each of life's seasons or situations provides the opportunity to learn more about God and His presence in our lives.

In the book of Acts, Paul and his travelling companions found themselves in a sticky situation and a difficult time in life and ministry. Paul was given a vision of a man standing and begging him to travel to Macedonia, help the people, and preach the gospel to them. Paul knew that God wanted him to travel to the region (Acts 16:8–10).

Along the way, Paul and his companion, Silas, were thrown in prison for setting a woman free from an evil spirit. They were beaten and locked up. This was one of those times in life no one wants to sign up for. Yet look what happened next.

4. Read **Acts 16:16–25**. How did Paul and Silas respond to this inconvenient, uncomfortable, and unpleasant time in life? What surprises you most about Paul and Silas's response?

Paul and Silas were sentenced to flogging and prison for "teach[ing] customs which are not lawful for . . . Romans" (v. 21). Little did the accusers know that these two men were also Romans. The accusers assumed that Paul and Silas were of a different nationality and adhered to different customs, but both Paul and Silas were under Roman rule. Roman citizens would never have received the beating and treatment that these two received.

5. How do you tend to respond when you're faced with an inconvenient, uncomfortable, and unpleasant time in life? What can you learn from Paul and Silas's response?

The two men didn't complain or abandon the cause but began praising God in the middle of a difficult circumstance. In response, God did something miraculous.

6. Read **Acts 16:26–34**. How did God reveal Himself in the midst of the difficult situation Paul and Silas found themselves in?

The jailer desired the same faith as Paul and Silas and begged to know what he needed to do to be saved. Paul and Silas assured him that nothing needed to be done, but he should simply believe. Everything had already been done on his behalf by Christ.

7. When you're facing a difficult time in life, do you expect God to reveal Himself to you in an unexpected way? Why or why not?

On occasion, God allows us to experience undesirable times or situations in life, but He remains with us. Even in those times we can choose to call out to God and worship Him in the midst.

8. Reflecting on the season that you're in, what do you think God is revealing about Himself to you? What opportunities do you have to call out to God and worship Him?

Every
season of life
provides an opportunity to
learn something more about God.
Though we don't always get to choose
our season of life, we can always choose
to call out to God and worship
Him in the midst.

Digging Deeper

Few people in the world can compare their difficult time with Job's—a man stripped of all his possessions, many of his loved ones, and even his health. The first thirty-seven chapters of Job describe Job and his friends wrestling theologically over why Job had to suffer. Starting in Job 38, God's response revealed He cannot be contained in a theological box. Read **Job 38:1–18**. How would you have responded if you were Job and God was asking you all of these questions? What comfort do you find in knowing that God created all things and holds all things together? Spend some time thanking God for His tender care of the minutest details of your life.

Bonus Activity

Spend fifteen minutes each day this upcoming week worshiping God.
Before you log on to the computer or snuggle in for a good night's sleep,
turn on your favorite worship album. Sing praises to God or read the
words to your favorite hymn. Write prayers in a journal or enjoy time
in nature. Spend time reflecting on how God is revealing Himself to
you during this season and praise Him for what He is doing—seen and
unseen—today and every day.

A time to be born.

Ecclesiastes 3:2

A Time for New Beginnings

Called to Something Fresh

Have you ever heard the term *foodie*? Maybe the word describes you! The term refers to anyone who is both particular and passionate about his or her culinary selections.

Many foodies will go to extremes by driving dozens (and even hundreds!) of miles to visit a specific restaurant for a single item on the menu. Some foodies will order their spices from boutique shops and refuse to purchase their meats or vegetables from anywhere but a specific store. Every foodie is unique, but they all share a love for a great meal.

But what happens when a foodie decides to feed those in the local community?

Something amazing!

Michael Blewett, pastor of Christ Episcopal Church in Bowling Green, Kentucky, has decided he doesn't want to leave his passion for food at home and instead brings it right into the church and local community. On Wednesdays, Christ Episcopal Church opens its doors to those who are hungry. They serve everyone from bankers to bums, from the highfalutin to the homeless. But don't expect mystery casserole or save-the-scraps soup. Instead, Michael and his volunteers serve home-cooked, made-from-scratch, gourmet-style meals to the community. They serve a wide range of fresh, colorful dishes including finely chopped vegetables, high-end chili, grilled meats, and tasty stews.

One of the most exciting things about being a child of God is that God is always up to something new.

Those who attend a meal don't stand in a traditional buffet line, but rather order from a menu. Michael says it isn't unusual for those who are homeless in the community to call on Tuesday night to find out what's going to be on the menu the next day. And the regulars know to get there early, because the most popular items always run out fast.

The experience is enriching for everyone involved. Everyone from the community is welcome, so the meal provides an opportunity for those with resources and those without to build friendships. Each person who attends is fed both physically and spiritually.

Michael and the Christ Episcopal Church didn't set out to do something new and different simply for the sake of being new or different. They saw a need and used their unique passions, gifts, and talents to create a new twist on serving those in the community.

Their story reminds us that sometimes God uses us and the community we're in to do something new to share the love of Christ with others. Indeed, God uses people in all kinds of innovative ways to spread His love and bring Him glory. God loves to work through us.

But sometimes the new thing God is doing is within us. Through the Holy Spirit, God may work in our lives in such a way that we see Him, others, or even ourselves in a fresh way. One of the most exciting things about being a child of God is that God is always up to something new.

1. Does the idea of innovation or trying something new tend to invigorate you or make you nervous? Mark your answer on the continuum below. Explain your response to the group.

●━━━━━━━━━━━━━━━━━━━━━━━━━━━━━━━━━━━━●

Innovation makes me nervous　　　　　**Innovation invigorates me**

2. Describe a time that you've been part of a ministry, outreach, or church that tried something creative or new to spread the love of Christ to others. What did you discover about yourself and others through the experience?

Sometimes stepping out in faith to be part of something new that God is doing stretches us beyond our comfort zones. This was particularly true for Moses. While tending the flock of his father-in-law, Moses came upon a fiery bush that refused to burn up. Intrigued by the marvelous sight, Moses turned aside. When he did, God called to him from the midst of the bush.

While shepherding was a common profession in the ancient Near East, one can't miss the double meaning in Moses' job. He not only shepherded sheep but would become the shepherd for God's people as he led them out of Egypt and into the promised land.

3. Read **Exodus 3:1–10**. What new things did God want to do for the Israelites through Moses?

From the fiery bush, God told Moses to remove his sandals. This practice of reverence was an ancient Near Eastern practice still used today.

4. Read **Exodus 3:11–15** and **Exodus 4:1–17**. In the chart below, note each of Moses' concerns and how God responded to each one.

Scripture	Moses' Concern	God's Response
Exodus 3:11, 12		
Exodus 3:13–15		
Exodus 4:1–9		
Exodus 4:10–12		
Exodus 4:13–17		

How do you think you would have responded to God if you were Moses?

God's response to Moses revealed His ways are often much different than our own. Despite our protests that something won't work or somehow we're not qualified, if God calls us to do something new He will provide a way.

5. Whom do you know that's doing something new or innovative to spread the love of Jesus to others? What inspires you most about his or her work? How can you be a voice of encouragement and support in this person's life?

Moses' reluctant leadership displayed God's greatness. Through an unlikely shepherd, God saved an entire nation. The glory can be given to God alone.

6. In what area of your life do you sense the Holy Spirit nudging you to step out and try something new, or even new-to-you, in order to spread the love of Christ? What's stopping you from responding?

Not only does God do new things *through* us but He also does new things *within* us. God is steadily renewing us—or making us new—as we yield to Him in our lives.

The apostle Paul wrote two letters to the church in Corinth. The letter that modern Bibles call Second Corinthians addressed the purity of God's people. Paul described the restoration of God's people as reflective of the greater restoration of creation brought through Jesus.

7. Read **2 Corinthians 5:17**. What new work is done within us when we choose to give our lives to Christ?

8. How did you experience this passage to be true in your life when you first gave your life to Christ? How have you experienced this passage to be true on an ongoing basis?

God is in the business of making all things new. Sometimes God uses the community that we're in to do something new to share the love of Christ with others. Other times God wants to do something new within us. Both can make us more Christlike.

Digging Deeper

Because of their disobedience to God, the Israelites found themselves in captivity in a foreign nation. During this time, the book of Lamentations was penned. Read **Lamentations 3:19-23**. When are you most tempted to begin doubting the lovingkindness and compassion of God? How have you found this passage to be true in your life? How does this passage give you hope?

Bonus Activity

Consider how participants going through this study together can do something new to spread the love of Christ to others in the local community. Whether serving a meal, delivering gifts, or offering encouraging words, try something new as a group to spread and celebrate Christ's love during the upcoming week.

A time to die.

Ecclesiastes 3:2

A Time for Necessary Endings

Leaving Behind the Familiar

Born in 1848, Mary Slessor was raised by an alcoholic father. When she grew older, she found work in a cotton mill, but she longed to become a missionary. She found inspiration in David Livingstone, an early nineteenth century British explorer who traveled to remote regions in Africa to share the good news of Jesus Christ. Compelled by his story, Mary left her home in order to go where no other white person had settled in Western Africa.

At the age of twenty-eight, Mary established a missionary base in the Calabar region of Africa. Settling in the area was highly dangerous. Some of the accepted cultural beliefs of the time included burying widows alive in their husbands' graves and killing innocent children. Yet Mary refused to give up—despite battling sickness often and living with constant threats. Over the years, her commitment to Christ, sharing the gospel, and opposing injustices had a profound impact on the culture. Not only did locals hear the good news of Jesus Christ but Mary challenged a long-held superstition that twins were evil. Because of her hard work and prayer, locals finally quit the horrible customary practice of killing and abandoning twins.

Today in Nigeria, Mary is recognized and honored as a spiritual leader who saved the lives of countless children and women and shared the good news of Christ with many.[1]

God used a short, red-haired, Presbyterian missionary to make a profound impact in our world. But in order to lay hold of the life God had for Mary Slessor, she had to leave that which was comfortable and familiar behind, a necessary ending, in order to lay hold of the new beginning God had for her. Though our stories may not be as dramatic as Mary's, we all have moments in our lives when we sense God calling us to leave something behind in order to lay hold of the something new God has for us. Sometimes the necessary endings we're facing are practical. We may sense the invitation to leave a place or a job in order to step into the fullness of life and service God intends. Or we may feel a nudge toward a necessary ending through forgiveness of something that happened to us in the past. Or maybe we're aware of an unhealthy pattern or addiction in our lives and we've got to make a break.

Whatever necessary ending you may need to make, rest assured that it's worth it in order to lay hold of the freedom and fullness of life God has for you.

All of us will encounter moments of necessary endings.

> We all have moments in our lives when we sense God calling us to leave something behind in order to lay hold of the something new God has for us.

1. When in your life have you made a significant change, a necessary ending, and discovered God had a new beginning waiting for you?

2. When you're facing a necessary ending, what is the most difficult aspect for you emotionally? Physically? Spiritually?

Sometimes we must let go and move on from that which is familiar in order to embrace all God has for us. One of the ways the disciples did this was by leaving behind all they knew to follow Christ. They accepted the necessary ending of what they knew in order to lay hold of the new beginning as disciples of Jesus.

Levi, also known as Matthew, was a man with a good job with great income. But Jesus had more to offer this tax collector. Jesus invited Levi to the new beginning of a lifetime.

3. Read **Luke 5:27, 28**. How did Levi respond to Jesus' invitation? What have you left behind in order to become a follower of Christ? What has made this decision worthwhile?

One of the great paradoxes or upside down principles of following Jesus is that when we choose to die to ourselves through the grace of the Holy Spirit, then we become more alive to Christ. Jesus illustrated this idea through His life, death, and resurrection and also through His teaching.

4. Read **Matthew 16:24, 25**. When have you tried holding on to your life but discovered that God had something more for you?

When Jesus spoke the words in Matthew 16, the disciples were all too familiar with witnessing rebels carrying Roman crosses to the place where they would be crucified. The idea of carrying a cross was all too real of a possibility to the disciples or anyone who opposed the government. But the cross analogy evoked a two-fold meaning: carrying one's cross represented the willingness to deny oneself as well as willingness to die for Christ.

Throughout the Gospels Jesus often said that His hour to die had not yet come. However, in John 12, Jesus finally declared that the hour had arrived. Jesus pointed to this as the hour of glorification—the time for Him to be crucified, buried, and risen. Jesus would lay down His life to bring redemption to the world. Through Jesus' death, He offered new life to many.

5. Read **John 12:23–26**. How willing are you to sacrifice for the sake of others? In what way have you seen the truth of the principle that through self-sacrifice comes new life?

Laying down our lives for someone else is the ultimate sign of love, affection, and friendship. While Jesus' sacrifice led to new life for those who believe, our own sacrifices are necessary so that we may have life ourselves. The apostle John described a bad example of showing love in 1 John 3:11–15. In contrast, he illustrated the perfect example through Jesus Christ.

6. Read **1 John 3:16**. When in the last year have you experienced someone laying down his or her life to make a meaningful sacrifice for you? How did his or her actions make Christ's sacrifice more real to you?

Greek, the original language for most of the New Testament, has more than one word for "life." *Bios* is the earthly life, from which we derive the words "biology" or "biosphere," and *zoe* is the new life offered by God. We are called to lay down our *bios* to receive the *zoe* that God has in store.

7. When in the last year have you laid down your life and made a meaningful sacrifice for someone else? What did you discover about yourself through that experience? What did you discover about God?

8. What necessary endings do you sense God nudging you toward in your life? What's stopping you from making those necessary endings?

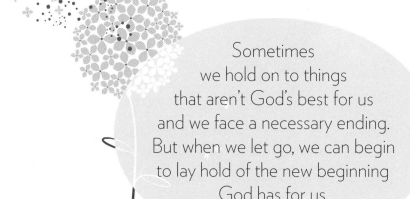

Sometimes
we hold on to things
that aren't God's best for us
and we face a necessary ending.
But when we let go, we can begin
to lay hold of the new beginning
God has for us.

Digging Deeper

Read **Genesis 13:5–18**. What necessary ending did Abram (Abraham) face in his relationship with Lot? How did Abram respond to the situation? How did God reward Abram for his response? What wisdom or hope did Abram's story give you in any necessary endings that you're facing in your life?

Bonus Activity

Reflecting on this lesson, consider any necessary endings you sense God nudging you toward in your life. Over the course of the next week, prayerfully consider what moving toward one of these changes might look like. On a calendar, establish a timeline for these changes. Consider asking a friend to pray for and encourage you along the way.

A time to plant,
And a time to pluck what is planted.

Ecclesiastes 3:2

A Time to Transition

The Importance of Change

For some of us change is easy. We love the excitement of trying something new, stepping out of our comfort zone, and experiencing a new activity. Without something new, we tend to grow bored and disengaged. But for others of us, change makes us uneasy. We are more comfortable with the familiar and predictable. When life is steady, we're able to not only come alive but thrive.

Whether you're a fan of change or one who tries to resist it at all costs, everyone inevitably faces seasons of transition in life. What's your response? Take the How Do You Respond to Change? Quiz to find out:

✤ How Do You Respond to Change? Quiz

1. You've planned to grab lunch with one of your best girlfriends at your favorite restaurant. You've had the lunch date on your calendar for more than two weeks. But on the way to the restaurant she calls and says she can't make the appointment. You respond by:

   a) Bemoaning her cancellation and questioning the details of why she won't be able to meet you. You feel like your day is ruined.

   b) Gently asking if you can do anything to help her day go better and finding out when she can reschedule.

   c) Telling her that it's no problem and you two will get a date on the calendar soon. Without missing a beat, you run through your phone list to see who else might be able to grab a last-minute lunch with you.

2. You've invited a couple you know to go out for an afternoon together. When they arrive at your door, you discover that they've brought three more people with them. You respond by:

   a) Trying not to let your exasperation about the situation show. You work hard to keep your cool regarding the uninvited and unexpected guests.

   b) Waiting for a free moment with one of your friends to find out why the three people came. Once you understand the situation, you make the best of the circumstances.

   c) Recognizing that your friends have provided the perfect opportunity for a small party. You're excited about the unexpected surprise.

3. The music minister at your church decides that instead of singing familiar songs and hymns he's going to spend the next month introducing the congregation to all new tunes. You respond by:

a) Letting the pastor and worship leader know how important the well-known, beloved songs are to you and the congregation. After church, you solicit the help of a few friends to share similar concerns with the church leaders.

b) Recognizing that learning new songs is sometimes difficult, but committing to hang in there for the next month and hope to learn something new.

c) Celebrating the new music being sung in your church and the opportunity to learn fresh songs.

4. The grocery store you always shop in has been closed for renovation. When the store reopens you discover none of the items are where they used to be. You respond by:

a) Complaining to the manager and then shopping at another grocery store you're more familiar with.

b) Spending a few weeks studying the store's new layout and asking a clerk to help you find specific items.

c) Loving the new layout and design. You can't wait to tell all your friends about the changes.

✤ Scoring:

Tally up the total number of A's, B's, and C's.
If you answered mostly A's, then you're a natural fan of consistency in your life. When change comes, you may be hesitant to try new things. But your friends probably find you rock solid and a source of stability. While it may be a challenge at first, reminding yourself that change

will inevitably happen may help you to minimize the stress you experience as a result of change.

If you answered mostly B's, then you have both an appreciation for consistency and an ability to embrace change in moderation. You've learned how to be flexible no matter what life brings you.

If you answered mostly C's, then you likely thrive whenever change is in the air. You love trying new things, exploring new places, and learning about almost anything new.

Whether you're a fan of change or one why tries to resist it at all costs, everyone inevitably faces seasons of transition in life. How will you respond?

No matter your natural response to change, the book of Ecclesiastes reminds us that a time under the sun exists for everything—including planting and uprooting. Sometimes we find ourselves in a season of planting—a time when we stay in one place, root deeper in our relationships and community, and embrace the stability that naturally comes. But other times we find ourselves in a season of uprooting—a time when change is taking place all around, even within us. Whatever season you find yourself in, rest assured that God is with you and He longs to see you flourish and to bring you to an even more fruitful life in Him.

1. What surprised you or caught your attention about your personal results to the How Do You Respond to Change Quiz? What is the hardest part about change for you?

In the book of Genesis, we discover the story of Joseph, a man who was planted and uprooted many times. Growing up as one of twelve kids, Joseph lived on the receiving end of constant ridicule from his brothers. Joseph had the gift of interpreting dreams and was his dad's favorite son. To show his favor, his dad even gave Joseph a coat covered in brilliant colors.

As if they weren't already jealous enough of Joseph's favorite son status, the brothers' jealousy reached a fever pitch when a well-intentioned Joseph told them of a dream he had that one day they would bow down to him. Fed up, the brothers sold Joseph into slavery, assuming they'd never hear from him again. Incredibly, after an adventure of triumphs and trials, Joseph wound up as second in command to Pharaoh, the king of Egypt.

During his time in Egypt, Joseph interpreted the king's dreams. God gave him the ability to see that there would be seven years of abundance followed by seven years of famine. The Egyptians were then able to gather and save during the years of abundance and to portion during the years of famine. But during the famine, Joseph's brothers came begging for help. Much to their surprise, the brother they abandoned was now Pharaoh's right-hand man. After mercy and forgiveness were extended, Joseph and Pharaoh invited Joseph's family to come live in Egypt so they might survive the years of famine.

2. Read **Genesis 47:1–12**. How did Joseph's father, Jacob (also known as Israel), and his family respond to the opportunity to settle in Goshen in the midst of a famine?

The Israelites remained in Egypt for many years and multiplied in abundance. They were fulfilling the creation mandate: to be fruitful and increase in number (Genesis 1:28). Some scholars estimate the Israelites stayed in Egypt for over four hundred years—long after Joseph and his brothers passed away.

3. Read **Exodus 1:1–7**. How were Joseph and his descendants blessed as they settled and put down roots in the area?

4. Describe a time in the past when you sensed God's blessing and provision as you put down roots in a new location, job, or stage in life. How did you know that God was with you during the time of transition?

The scene in Egypt changed for the Israelites after years of thriving. Though God brought Joseph, his family, and his descendants to Egypt, they could no longer stay if they were going to flourish. The Israelites' growth became threatening to the new Pharaoh in charge. The new Pharaoh feared Israel and ultimately became an enemy of God.

5. Read **Exodus 1:8–22**. What made the descendants of Joseph and his father, Jacob, known as the Israelites, want to uproot and leave Egypt?

The closing of Genesis set the scene for the changes the Israelites were about to face in the book of Exodus. After the Israelites settled in Goshen and experienced provision and growth, a new ruler took over Egypt who didn't treat the Israelites with kindness. The Israelites had to leave. Exodus is the tale of their journey out of Egypt and toward the promised land God had for them. In order to flourish again, they needed to uproot themselves from everything that was familiar. Throughout the long and difficult journey God reminded the people that He was with them time and time again.

6. When in the last year have you realized you needed to be uprooted from the place you'd been planted? How did you navigate the transition? What did you discover about God through the process?

No matter what transition we're facing, we can find comfort knowing that God is with us. In fact, one of God's names is "Alpha and Omega," the first and last letters of the Greek alphabet. The name symbolizes that God is the beginning and the end of all things, but also implies that He is with us in the middle.

7. Read **Revelation 1:8** and **Revelation 22:13**. Which is more meaningful in your own life—the idea that God is with you or the idea that God goes before you? Why?

8. What potential transitions are you facing in your relationships, workplace, finances, or living situation? In what areas is God inviting you to trust Him more during this time of transition?

Change isn't easy for most people. But rest assured that whenever you face a time of transition, God is with you. He longs to see you flourish and to bring you to a more fruitful life in Him.

Digging Deeper

Read **Luke 24:13–35**. Sometimes change is hard to wrap our minds around. This was particularly true after Jesus' death and resurrection, when many of His followers wondered what happened. How did Jesus meet His followers and help them understand what took place? When you're facing times of transition, what role do prayer and Scripture play in helping you make sense of what's happening?

Bonus Activity

Reflecting on this lesson, consider the potential transitions you're facing in your life. Consider writing them down on a piece of paper. Then ask God to reveal Himself in the midst of each one as the Alpha and Omega—the God who goes before you and with you every step of the way.

A time to heal.

Ecclesiastes 3:3

A Time to Heal
Hope for the Wounded

Have you ever scraped yourself and looked down only to be surprised by the amount of blood? The injury may not have been painful at the time, but suddenly you're looking at a wound that needs a bandage fast.

The goals of any first aid effort include protecting a person's life and giving the wound the best chance of healing quickly. But every wound heals differently. The person's age and health as well as the size and location of the cut and its susceptibility to infection all affect a wound's ability to heal. Plus, some people simply heal faster than others.

While wounds on our physical bodies may take a while to heal and may leave scars, the wounds on the inside—those unseen— often are the hardest to overcome and heal. The physical wounds can be alleviated with modern first aid practices or a trip to the doctor, but the wounds on the inside, whether emotional or relational, can be more complicated to heal.

All of us have been through hard times in life. Maybe we had to make a tough choice and we felt like something inside of us died. Maybe someone said something to us that cut us to the core. Maybe we experienced a loss or moment of pain that left us torn apart. We live in a fallen and imperfect world, and sometimes life throws painful punches.

But the good news is that God draws near to those who are wounded and brokenhearted. God not only remains with us but longs to renew us. God's first aid kit looks a bit different than a medical first aid kit. Instead of using gauze and antiseptic, God draws near us with His presence. Through the Holy Spirit, God comforts and encourages and heals us in areas of our souls and spirits that medical science can't explain.

God draws near to those who are wounded and broken- hearted.

Just as physical wounds heal in different ways over different time frames, God's healing touch in each of our lives differs as well. For some, God's healing may come in a single moment, but for others it may come over a span of months or years. God is the Great Physician of our souls and we can entrust ourselves wholly to Him.

1. Which do you tend to heal from more quickly, the scrapes and bruises of life that people can see or the scrapes and bruises of life that people can't see? Explain.

Throughout His life and ministry on earth, Jesus healed many people. The eyes of the blind were opened. The deaf heard. The crippled walked. Jesus healed not only people's physical bodies, He brought healing to their hearts and minds. That's important to remember because God doesn't limit healing to our physical bodies, but He also wants to heal our hearts and emotions.

The theme of Psalm 147 is a prayer to restore Israel's main city: Jerusalem. The psalmist began by praising God for His wondrous works of healing and restoration. God was physically restoring the city, but He was also healing the people emotionally and spiritually.

2. Read **Psalm 147**. When in your life have you experienced God as Healer of your emotions (v. 3)?

In the Old Testament, one of God's names is *Jehovah Rapha*, which translates to "The Lord Who Heals." In Exodus 15, God led His people, the Israelites, into the wilderness. As they desperately searched for water in the desert, God miraculously provided. In the wondrous provision, God promised not to plague the Israelites like He did the Egyptians in Exodus 7:14—11:10.

3. Read **Exodus 15:22–26**. What steps did the Israelites have to take to experience God as their Healer?

4. Look up the following passages. According to each passage, what are some examples of the healing available to us from God?

Scripture	Healing Available to Us
Psalm 41:4	
Jeremiah 3:22	
Luke 4:18	

5. Which of the areas listed in the chart above do you most long for God to heal in your life?

God knows that we need healing in many different areas of our lives. One of the great moments we have to look forward to is described in Revelation. In the new heaven, God will have trees specifically designed for spiritual healing.

6. Read **Revelation 22:1–5**. What comfort do you find knowing this is a snapshot of heaven?

The prophetic book of Ezekiel describes God's desire to restore Israel during their exile in Babylon. But a new king wasn't going to do the trick. Instead, Israel was in need of a full, head-to-toe makeover. God promised to heal them from the inside out.

7. Read **Ezekiel 36:26**. What new work does God long to do within us according to this passage?

8. Spend some time as a group sharing areas in your life—physical, spiritual, emotional, relational, or others—that need God's healing touch. Spend time praying together and asking God for His healing in each of these areas.

> God longs to bring healing and restoration in every area of our lives. We can entrust ourselves to God as our Healer.

Digging Deeper

Read **Mark 6:30–32**. Jesus instructed His disciples to come away from the hustle and bustle of life and ministry in order to be restored. What role does rest have in your own ability to experience God's restoration and healing? In your life, do you tend to heal more quickly when you stay busy or take time to rest? In what area of your life do you sense God nudging you to embrace rest more?

Bonus Activity

Reflecting on this lesson, make a list of people you know who need healing, whether physical, emotional, or relational. Each day this week, pray for the people on your list and consider dropping them a note of encouragement in the mail.

A time to break down,
And a time to build up.

Ecclesiastes 3:3

A Time
to Reassess

Breaking Down and Building Up

One of the most popular paintings of all time is Leonardo da Vinci's *The Last Supper*. The fifteenth-century mural depicts the scene of the final meal Jesus shared with His disciples before His arrest, trial, and crucifixion.

In 1977, Pinin Brambilla Barcilon was selected to lead the restoration project for this famous painting found on a monastery wall in Milan, Italy. The project was challenging, not just because of the artwork's size but its depth. Da Vinci's original choice of paint mixture was unstable and had begun flaking off before his death. Unprotected from humidity and pollution, the work continued to deteriorate for more than five centuries with mold, candle soot, and dust taking a heavy toll.

But the biggest challenge for Barcilon and her team was working through previous efforts of restoration. For more than three hundred years, amateur painters tried to update Da Vinci's work using wax, glue, varnish, and their own efforts to fill in gaping holes in the original artwork. The images became increasingly distorted. The details blurred.

When Barcilon's team approached *The Last Supper*, they knew they had their work cut out for them. They began photographing every detail of the image and analyzing the artwork with the latest technology. Then, they used microscopes to carefully remove the process of the damaged layers of over-painting. The process took twenty years. But eventually they began to discover the intensity of Da Vinci's brilliant brushstrokes. Matthew's hair turned out to be blonde instead of black. Thomas now had a left hand. Andrew's face depicted astonishment instead of sadness. And Jesus' face was illuminated by a fresh glow. Though the basic scene remained the same, the process of reassessing the original artwork and restoring *The Last Supper* brought the artwork alive in a captivating, powerful way.[1]

Sometimes in our lives we, too, go through seasons where we need to reassess. We may have areas of our personal lives, work, relationships, finances, or life trajectory in which we need to stop, pause, and see if we're still on track for what God has designed for us. We may discover areas that need to be touched up or reworked like the famous painting.

In the book of Ecclesiastes, Solomon declared there was "a time to break down, and a time to build up" (3:3). But knowing what season we're in—a time to downsize or a time to expand—requires us to seek God. As we reflect on where we've been and where God is leading us, we may need to reassess. In the process, we may discover God has a plan that's wildly different from anything we anticipated. But as we respond to His

> We may have areas of our personal lives, work, relationships, finances, or life trajectory in which we need to stop, pause, and see if we're still on track for what God has designed for us.

leading, we'll find—much like *The Last Supper*—the work God is doing in and through us is more beautiful that we ever imagined.

1. How often do you tend to reassess an aspect of your life? Mark the spot on the line that illustrates how often you do so. What aspects of your life do you tend to reassess the most? Why?

●━━━━━━━━━━━━━━━━━━━━━━━━━━━━━━━━━━━━━━━●

Every hour   **Every decade**

2. What areas of your life are you least likely to submit to God for reassessment?

Sometimes we are motivated to reevaluate as a type of general self-evaluation. But sometimes God nudges us to reassess a specific area of our lives. In the process, we may discover that God is calling us to tear down or downsize, or God may be calling us into a season of building and doing something new.

3. Read **Isaiah 55:8, 9**. When in your life have you specifically discovered that your plans vary from God's plans?

The book of Judges tells the story of Gideon, an unsuspecting man whose specific mission involved both starting something new and downsizing. God had given the Israelites into the hands of the Midianites for seven years because of the Israelites' disobedience. The name "Midian" means "strife," and these people were known to cause the Israelites all kinds of problems.

The Midianites stole and destroyed Israelite crops, killed livestock, and left Israel in complete poverty. Finally, the Israelites cried out to God for help and the Lord raised up an unlikely man named Gideon to help deliver them.

4. Read **Judges 6:11–16**. When has God asked you to start something new in a way that didn't, at first, make sense? What was the result?

Gideon didn't feel like a brave warrior. He felt insignificant and incapable. But God called Gideon to reassess the situation through His eyes. God reminded Gideon that He was with him and provided Gideon with a sign of His presence (Judges 6:17–24) despite Gideon's doubts and insecurities. In Judges 7, God asked Gideon to reassess the situation in a most unexpected way.

5. Read **Judges 7:1–8**. How did God ask Gideon to reassess his military force (hint: Deuteronomy 20:1–8)? When has God asked you to downsize in a way that, at first, didn't make sense to you? What was the result?

Gideon's fear and insecurities outweighed the signs God showed him. God continued revealing to Gideon that He was sovereign and encouraged Gideon in the fight against Midian. God would be the reason the Israelites won the battle—not Gideon's leadership or the tenacity of the army.

6. Read **Judges 7:9–15**. How did God's encouragement prepare Gideon for his mission (hint: v. 9)? When have you sensed God sending encouragement to you for something He has called you to do?

After wrestling over whether or not to trust God, Gideon determined to place his trust in God. Gideon knew that only through God could three hundred men defeat an army described to be as numerous as swarms of locusts. As a result, God rewarded Gideon's trust.

7. Read **Judges 7:16–21**. What was the result of Gideon's and his army's courage and obedience?

8. How are you discovering that God's ways are better than your ways?

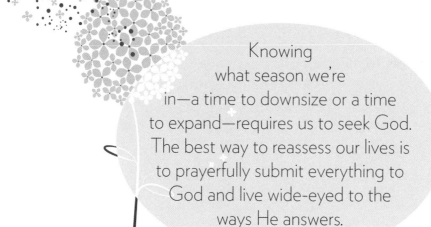

Knowing
what season we're
in—a time to downsize or a time
to expand—requires us to seek God.
The best way to reassess our lives is
to prayerfully submit everything to
God and live wide-eyed to the
ways He answers.

Digging Deeper

Read **James 1:5** and **Psalm 18:30**. What do each of these passages promise about God? How do these passages encourage you to submit every area of your life to God?

Bonus Activity

Over the course of the upcoming week, go online and look for a picture of *The Last Supper* or check out a book from your local library on this masterpiece. Take time to enjoy this artwork while you read **Luke 22:7–13**. Reflect on how a time to break down and a time to build up was demonstrated in the life of Christ.

Finding God in Every Season of Life

Often when we
face the challenging
seasons in life we
may forget that God
is right there with us.
He promises to fill us with
His grace, courage, strength,
compassion, and love along
the way. As we journey
toward becoming more and
more like Christ, we find that
our prayers become more
powerful, our rest more
rejuvenating, and our faith
more rewarding.

A time to weep,
And a time to laugh;
A time to mourn,
And a time to dance.

Ecclesiastes 3:4

A Time to Remain Faithful

Continuing Through Hardship

Elizabeth and Zacharias are one of the most remarkable couples in the Bible. Both are noted for being righteous before God (Luke 1:6). Yet despite their faithfulness, the couple struggled with infertility. As the years passed, they felt the pangs of unanswered prayer and the social disgrace of infertility that was prevalent in ancient culture. Eventually their hope for a child faded.

Yet Elizabeth and Zacharias remained faithful to God. Zacharias continued working in the temple as a priest. A time came when lots were cast among the thousands of priests to determine who would enter the temple's Holy Place to offer incense to God for the people. Zacharias's name was selected, providing him a once-in-a-lifetime opportunity and honor.

When Zacharias entered the Holy Place, he was shocked to see an angel. The angel encouraged Zacharias that he and

Elizabeth would become pregnant. Their son would become a forerunner to the long-awaited Messiah, and he would be called John.

Zacharias was taken aback by the news; he questioned the angel in disbelief. How could an old couple become fertile again? In the wake of Zacharias's doubts, the angel declared that Zacharias would not be able to speak until after the child was born. Zacharias left the temple able to communicate only through hand signals and drawings. Everyone knew something significant had taken place in the temple, but they'd have to wait to find out the news.

We can trust that God can transform our most painful and difficult areas into emblems of beauty and inspiring stories of restoration.

Elizabeth soon became pregnant. When the child was born, the couple's friends celebrated with great joy. On the eighth day, the time to circumcise and name the child, those present thought the child's name would be Zacharias after his dad. But Elizabeth protested and said the boy's name would be John. Zacharias confirmed Elizabeth's request by writing the same name on a tablet. Immediately, Zacharias's mouth was opened and he could speak again. After many long months of silence, his first words were praises to God. One can only imagine the joy, delight, and excitement the couple felt.

In all of our lives, we will experience moments of sadness and loss, as well as seasons of hope and joy. As Solomon acknowledged, there is "a time to weep, and a time to laugh; a time to mourn, and a time to dance" (Ecclesiastes 3:4). But no matter what season of life we're in—whether marked by hardship and pain or great joy and celebration—we can remain true and faithful to God even in the midst of our experience, as did Zacharias and Elizabeth. Some of the struggles we face in this life will challenge our faith, but we can choose to continue pursuing, seeking, and honoring God. We can trust that God can transform our most painful and difficult areas into emblems of beauty and inspiring stories of restoration.

1. When in the last year have you experienced each of these seasons in your life?

Season of Life	Specific Moment You Experienced
A time to weep	(e.g. death of a loved one)
A time to laugh	
A time to mourn	
A time to dance	

2. Reflecting on the specific moments you experienced, how did God reveal that He was with you in each one?

Elizabeth's name meant "dedicated to God" and Zacharias's name meant "God has remembered." Some Bible translations may use Zechariah (the Hebrew version) or Zacharias (the Greek version). Their story is one of a couple who was dedicated to God and whom God remembered.

3. Read **Luke 1:1–25**. How do you think Zacharias and Elizabeth stayed faithful during all the years of waiting? What has helped you stay faithful during your years of waiting on God?

4. Read **Luke 1:57–66**. Which of the following emotions do you think Zacharias and Elizabeth felt about everything from their infertility to encountering the angel to having the promised child? Place a check by each one.

_____ Mourning/Weeping	_____ Gratitude
_____ Sorrow	_____ Elation/Laughter
_____ Embarrassment	_____ Joy
_____ Shame	_____ Helplessness
_____ Disappointment	_____ Fear
_____ Shock	_____ Awe

5. When you faced a season of waiting on God, which of the emotions listed above did you experience? What emotions would you add?

Psalm 30 is known as a lament psalm and a psalm of thanksgiving. Lament psalms are poems in which the author cries out to God for deliverance. Attributed to King David, the psalm's words described knowing God intimately—as well as feeling distant from Him. David's song portrayed seasons of mountaintop experiences with God and times of dark valleys. Many of us can relate to the array of emotions David felt. We are reminded that even when God seems distant, we can still place our trust and hope in Him.

6. Read **Psalm 30**. What emotions are expressed in this psalm? Make a list in the space below.

Even when life seems tough, we can place our hope in God to come and turn our mourning into dancing. God alone has the power to turn our tears of sadness into tears of joy.

7. When have you experienced God transforming your mourning into dancing (Psalm 30:11)?

8. In what areas of your life do you need God to transform your mourning into dancing? Spend some time praying for those who are waiting for their mourning to be transformed to dancing. Ask God for the strength and grace to remain faithful no matter what life brings.

Whether our current season of life is marked by hardship and pain or great joy and celebration, we can remain faithful knowing that God remains with us.

Digging Deeper

Read **Luke 4:16–20** and **Isaiah 61:1–3**. What's significant about Jesus reading from this passage from Isaiah as He began His earthly ministry? What comfort do you find knowing that this was Jesus' mission? How have you experienced Jesus in this way in your life?

Bonus Activity

Over the course of the next week, commit **Isaiah 61:1–3** to memory. Consider writing the verses on a note card or typing the scriptures as a text or email and sending them to yourself so you can study them throughout each day.

A time to cast away stones,
And a time to gather stones;
A time to embrace,
And a time to refrain from embracing.

Ecclesiastes 3:5

A Time for Fruitfulness and Replenishment

Gathering and Scattering

Discovering the beautiful rhythms of life means paying attention to timing—particularly when to say yes and when to say no and recognizing that God uses all seasons to help us become more fruitful. Perhaps that's part of what Solomon was trying to communicate when he wrote that there's "a time to cast away stones, and a time to gather stones; a time to embrace, and a time to refrain." God has the perfect timing for everything.

One of the sweetest reminders of this truth, that seasons of life call us to different activities, is tucked away in the book of Leviticus. In the midst of a long list of laws given to the people, the attention shifts toward agriculture—specifically fruit trees. In Leviticus 19:23–25, God told His people not to eat a tree's fruit until the fifth year. Why? During the first three years, the tree had the opportunity to bulk up the amount of fruit it produced. Then, the fourth year, the fruit harvest was given to God as a tithe or gift. Then, the fifth year, the fruit was picked and enjoyed by everyone.

In order to abide by this law, the Jewish people developed a collective date as every tree's birthday. This allowed the Jewish people to more easily keep track of their trees' ages. Today, this holiday is known as Tu B'Shevat or the Jewish New Year for Trees, and it's celebrated early every year.[1]

God has the perfect timing for everything.

In instructing the people not to gather the fruit, God wasn't trying to take something away from the people but give them something even better. A young tree didn't have the root structure or the limb support to provide a healthy harvest of plump juicy fruits. By instructing His people to wait three years before gathering the first crop, God gave ample time for the tree to build up the strength necessary to support fruit. In the long run, the tree was healthier, lived longer, and yielded a bigger crop of delectable delights all because the plant had time to bolster its roots.

Just as God has a plan that bolsters the fruitfulness of trees, He also has a plan to develop the fruitfulness in our lives. In some seasons of life, God will call us to gather—to become highly active and productive. In other seasons of life, God will call us to scatter—to become less active and productive so we can recover and become rejuvenated. Times of fruitfulness and replenishment are necessary in our lives if we're going to grow into all God has for us.

1. In your life right now, do you sense God has you in a season of productivity and fruitfulness or in a season of replenishing your roots and growing stronger? Explain.

2. Which season of life—productivity and fruitfulness or replenishing and strengthening—do you naturally prefer? Why?

Psalm 1 serves as the introduction for the rest of the book of Psalms. The song's words remind us of the wisdom and joy that come with being attentive to God's Word. On the other hand, we see the fruitlessness that comes with disobeying God's Word. Psalm 1 encourages us to dig our roots deep and drink in the sweet guidance of God's Word so that we may become fruitful and prosperous.

3. Read **Psalm 1**. Draw a picture of the tree described in this passage in the space below (hint: v. 3). Then add circles representing fruit. Fill in each circle with a fruit you've seen grow in your life.

4. According to this passage, what makes the difference between those who are well established and fruitful and those who are not?

The Gospel of Luke tells the story of Jesus visiting Mary and Martha. Martha worked hard to extend hospitality and prepare delicious meals for her guests. Mary sat with Jesus and hung on every one of His words. She didn't want to miss a moment of enjoying the company of her guests. Both sisters had very different approaches to the way they greeted, interacted with, and served Jesus in this scene.

5. Read **Luke 10:38–42**. What are some of the strengths of Martha's approach to serving Jesus?

6. What are some of the strengths of Mary's approach to serving Jesus?

7. On the continuum below, mark whether your approach to spending time with Jesus is more like Martha's or more like Mary's.

More like Martha's   **More like Mary's**

How do you grow in your faith when you take the approach that doesn't come naturally to you when spending time with Jesus?

Through service, we have the opportunity to grow in the ways we express our faith and become more fruitful. But we can't be highly productive in every moment of life. Sometimes we need to slow down and replenish our roots knowing that God is working then too.

8. In what areas of your life do you need to consider opportunities to serve and give to others? In what areas of your life do you need to slow down and replenish your roots? What's stopping you from making those changes?

Being fruitful as followers of Jesus requires seasons of productivity and seasons of replenishment. We can trust that God is at work no matter what season we're in.

Digging Deeper

The apostle Paul wrote a letter to the church in Corinth, in which he stated that Christian leaders were mere servants in comparison with God. Read **1 Corinthians 3:5–9**. According to this passage, regardless of what we do, who ultimately brings the growth? What comfort do you find knowing the true source of growth? Into what areas of your life do you need to ask God to bring growth or fruitfulness?

Bonus Activity

On a blank sheet of paper, make a list of the areas of your life that you'd like to be more fruitful. Spend some time in prayer asking God to increase fruitfulness in each of these areas. Be sensitive to any ways that God may be calling you to step back in one area in order to be more fruitful in another.

A time to gain,
And a time to lose;
A time to keep,
And a time to throw away;
A time to tear,
And a time to sew.

Ecclesiastes 3:6, 7

A Time for Resolutions

Following Through

Once we resolve to make a change in our lives—whether on January 1st or any other time of the year—what makes the difference in following through? Author and psychologist Richard Wiseman decided he wanted to find out. In 2007, he tracked over three thousand people committed to a wide range of personal resolutions from quitting smoking to becoming more physically active.

Through the study, Wiseman examined not just why so many people failed to make a change but what could be done to ensure their success. He discovered that women were most successful in keeping their resolutions when they told their friends and family about their goals and were encouraged to be resilient even when they reverted to old habits. These simple practices increased women's success by ten percent.

To keep a resolution, Wiseman advises, people should make only one resolution at a time. People are far more likely to succeed when they focus their attention and energy into one area of behavior. Planning ahead is also important. Last-minute resolutions are harder to keep than those that have been reflected on. Rather than focus efforts on a failed resolution from the past, make a new personal resolution or tackle the goal from a fresh angle. For example, instead of trying to lose a particular number of pounds, focus your efforts on gaining muscle strength. And be specific about the resolution. Vague or open-ended resolutions are much more difficult to keep than specific and deadline-oriented goals.[1]

Solomon hinted at some of the changes we need to make in our lives when he observed, "[There's] a time to gain, and a time to lose; a time to keep, and a time to throw away; a time to tear, and a time to sew."

Many of our resolutions revolve around these themes. Gaining new, healthy habits. Giving up some unhealthy ones. Keeping better track of finances and schedule. Cutting back on areas of over-commitment. Moving away from activities that drain energy and rekindling activities that bring life. Often the resolutions that we make circle around these themes of gaining, losing, keeping, tossing, tearing, and mending.

No matter what changes or resolution we sense the Holy Spirit leading us to make in our personal, spiritual, physical, relational, or professional lives, we don't have to make those changes on our own. God is with us. We can ask God to strengthen us, extend grace to us, and give us the courage to make any and every change we need so that we can walk in the fullness of all He has for us.

> No matter what changes or resolution we sense the Holy Spirit leading us to make . . . God is with us.

1. In what specific areas in your life do you sense God leading you to make a change, to let go, to hold on (despite the difficulty), to declutter or simplify, to develop healthy boundaries, or to heal a relationship in order to become more Christlike?

2. Reflecting on your responses, what one resolution will you choose to make in your life right now?

3. Consider how you can make your resolution more attainable by reflecting on the following areas:

   ✤ How can you make your resolution more reasonable by making it specific and measurable?

   ✤ What will you gain by achieving this goal?

   ✤ What small steps can you take to achieve your goal?

   ✤ What changes in your schedule could you make to attain your resolution?

   ✤ Who could you invite to encourage and support you in this goal?

   ✤ Now rewrite your specific resolution or goal in the space below.

Whenever we have an area of our life where we want to see a healthy change, we can seek God through prayer with the confidence that He hears us.

4. Look up the following passages. What does each one reveal about the power and effectiveness of prayer? Place a star by the passage most meaningful to you.

   Psalm 66:20:

   Isaiah 65:24:

   Matthew 21:22:

   Romans 8:26:

   James 5:16:

When we pray about the changes we want to make in our lives, we can trust God as the source of our strength.

5. Look up the following passages. What does each one reveal about the strength of God? Place a star by the passage that is most meaningful to you.

   1 Chronicles 16:11:

   Psalm 18:32–34:

   Isaiah 40:28–31:

   1 Corinthians 10:13:

   Philippians 4:13:

God doesn't just give us strength as we turn to Him; He also gives us grace. Grace is a free gift God offers us through the life, death, and resurrection of Jesus Christ. When Jesus died on the cross, He took the sins of the world on His shoulders and, through grace, gave us the opportunity of eternal life. God's grace envelops everything He offers us.

6. Look up the following passages. What does each one reveal about the grace God gives us? Place a star by the passage that is most meaningful to you.

Romans 5:21:

2 Corinthians 12:9:

Hebrews 4:16:

James 4:6:

2 Peter 1:2:

Throughout the Scriptures, God called people to make all kinds of changes—leading them into new lands, new adventures, and new areas where He was at work. Making these changes required courage. No matter what new thing God is calling you toward, He is the source of your courage.

7. Look up the following passages. What does each one reveal about the courage God gives us? Place a star by the passage that is most meaningful to you.

Deuteronomy 31:6:

Joshua 1:3–9:

Psalm 27:1:

Romans 8:15:

2 Timothy 1:7:

8. Reflecting on the scriptures highlighted in this lesson on the effectiveness of prayer and God as the source for strength, grace, and courage, are you ready to commit to the resolution you made in question 2 that will make you more Christlike? Why or why not?

Whenever we resolve to become more Christlike, we can seek God through prayer. He will strengthen us, extend grace to us, and provide the courage to make any necessary changes in our lives as we seek Him.

Digging Deeper

Zacchaeus was a man of short stature who had a hated profession—he was a chief tax collector who took money from his own people. Read **Luke 19:1–10**. What resolution or commitment to change did Zacchaeus want to make in his life? What motivated him to make this change? How did God provide the strength, grace, and courage to keep his resolution? What does this story reveal about the way God will meet us when we honestly seek Him?

Bonus Activity

Schedule a time to get together with your group or some other friends. Share your resolution with them and spend time working toward that goal together. If you want to spend more time in Scripture, then spend time reading God's Word as a group at a local coffee shop or tea place. Dive into discussion over yummy blueberry scones and a white mocha. If your resolution is to spend more time serving others, head to the local food bank or homeless shelter. As a group, spend time serving others and becoming more Christlike in the meantime. Pull out your calendars and fit in time monthly or even weekly to continue pursuing your resolution.

A time to keep silence,
And a time to speak.

Ecclesiastes 3:7

A Time for Silence and Speaking

The Value of Knowing the Difference

Queen Vashti wasn't having it. All her husband wanted to do was show off her beauty—not admire her intelligence, boldness, or kindness. One fate-filled night, she put her foot down and refused to come when summoned.

This set King Ahasuerus into a rage. He divorced Vashti and searched for a new beauty queen to marry. Young virgin women gathered from all over the country. After hosting a Ms. Persia pageant of sorts—including twelve months of beauty treatments for the contestants—the king's eyes grew big and his royal jaw dropped at the sight of a dark-haired knockout. He chose this young woman to be his new wife.

Esther came from humble beginnings. Orphaned at a young age, she was raised by her cousin Mordecai during the Exile—a time when all the Jews were forced to leave their land and enter into captivity. Instead of returning to Jerusalem at the end of the Exile as did most of the Jews, Esther and Mordecai chose to stay in Persia.

Esther, an orphaned, captured Jew, having been chosen by King Ahasuerus, became the Queen of Persia. Fearful of what the king might do, Mordecai forbade Esther from revealing her Jewish background. He suspected that admitting her true nationality would risk not only her crown but also Esther's life. Esther obeyed and remained silent.

Mordecai continued to check up on his cousin during her time in the palace. One day, outside of the city's gates, he refused to bow to the king's right-hand man, Haman, because Mordecai would bow to no one but God. Haman learned that Mordecai was a Jew and set his eyes on destroying not only Mordecai but all of the Jews. He began planting seeds of hate and destruction in the ear of King Ahasuerus. Soon, Ahasuerus ordered for all Jews—young and old, women and children—to be killed.

Mordecai heard of Haman's plan and wept for his people. Esther learned of Mordecai's distress and asked how she could help. Mordecai told her that she would have to approach the king—an act forbidden without summons. She would have to advocate on behalf of her people—to save the entire Jewish nation. She had to speak up.

Boldly, Esther approached the throne of her husband. She finally revealed her identity. She was a Jew and was destined to be murdered if the king continued with his decree.

The king immediately corrected what was made wrong and sentenced Haman to death. Mordecai replaced Haman as the king's right-hand man. He restored the freedom of the Jews—and gave them the ability to assemble and protect themselves. Because of Esther's boldness and bravery, an entire nation was saved. Jews across the country celebrated and rejoiced at the good news.

Today, Jews still celebrate the courage of Queen Esther in a yearly feast called Purim.

> Because of Esther's boldness and bravery, an entire nation was saved.

Most of us won't be called to marry royalty or to risk our lives to save others from genocide, but the story of Esther is a powerful reminder that there are times when we need to be silent and times when we need to speak up. Knowing the difference requires us to humbly seek God through prayer and ask for His wisdom, grace, and discernment.

1. Reflecting on the story of Esther, when in your life have you wondered why God allowed particular circumstances to happen but now you recognize that God was at work through them?

Interestingly enough, God's name is never mentioned in the book of Esther. God moves and works in invisible ways throughout the story of Esther. While God may not be mentioned specifically, He brought everything together for His glory.

2. Read **Esther 2:17–20** and **Esther 4:12–14**. When has God given you a position of influence in which silence was essential? When has God given you a position of influence in which speaking up was essential?

3. When in the last month have you spoken up about something and realized that you should not have said anything?

4. When in the last month have you remained silent about something and realized that you should have spoken up?

5. What do the following passages reveal about the importance of silence?

Psalm 34:13:

Proverbs 11:9:

Proverbs 11:12, 13:

James 1:26:

1 Peter 3:10:

6. What do the following passages reveal about the importance of speaking up?

John 3:11:

Romans 1:16:

Colossians 3:16:

1 Peter 3:15, 16:

Hebrews 13:15:

King Solomon's book of Proverbs offers wisdom on when to speak and when to hold our tongue. Our speech has a two-fold power: for good and for bad.

7. Read **Proverbs 18:21**. What role does God play in helping you discern when to speak and when to remain silent?

Proverbs 31:8, 9 says, "Open your mouth for the speechless, in the cause of all who are appointed to die. Open your mouth, judge righteously, and plead the cause of the poor and needy."

8. In what areas of your life do you sense God nudging you to remain silent? In what areas of your life do you sense God nudging you to speak up?

> Sometimes God calls us to speak up. Sometimes God calls us to remain silent. To discern the difference, we can seek God through prayer.

Digging Deeper

Read **James 3:3-12**. What three things does James compare the tongue—or speech—to? How have you found your speech to hold these positions of power in your own life and relationships? When has your speech led you into trouble? What good things result through our speech? How in the next week can you keep better rein on your speech?

Bonus Activity

Speak up for the voiceless. Select one of your favorite organizations. Use charitynavigator.org to learn about organizations in your area. Organize a fundraising event, find out how you can volunteer, and see what role you can play to begin speaking up for the voiceless.

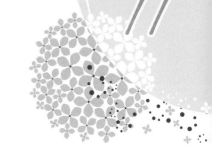

A time to love,
And a time to hate.

Ecclesiastes 3:8

A Time for Love

Reaching Out to Others

Martin Rowe grew up on a farm in rural Georgia. One day at age six, he was riding with his father on the tractor. As they were driving along, the machine flipped over. Martin and his father were taken to the hospital. Martin had damaged one arm and lost the use of the other completely.

The hospital bill totaled over $32,000.

The family wondered how they'd ever pay back that kind of debt. One day Martin heard his parents talking about the financial pressures. Martin assured his mom that he would pay off the bill himself. Though grateful for the support and concern, Martin's mom knew such ambitions were more fiction than reality for a small child.

Martin returned home and soon went back to school. After classes were dismissed each day, Martin walked along the side of the road and picked up glass bottles for recycling. A few months later, Martin had earned $400 with the recycled bottles. He presented the money to his mother who was in awe of her child's accomplishment.

But Martin had just begun his efforts. He soon learned that aluminum cans could also be redeemed for cash. His collection efforts grew. When a nearby aluminum company heard of Martin's efforts they agreed to donate their scrap metal. Another company joined in. For five years, Martin collected cans after school, and at the age of eleven, he paid off the $32,000 debt.[1]

A young child's story provides a glimpse into the power of big love. Martin Rowe, motivated by the big love he had for his parents, defied the odds and paid back an enormous debt. Though our stories may be very different from Martin's, we all have opportunities to love big. We all know people who are facing impossible situations. We may know an individual person or an entire family that needs to experience God's love and goodness in a profound way. And God will use us to express that love.

We all have opportunities to love big.

Solomon once wrote that there's a "time to love, and a time to hate" (Ecclesiastes 3:8). Thinking about a time to hate can trip us up. Solomon isn't saying that there's a time to be nasty or mean, but rather there are some things that are simply wrong in our world—like injustice and abuse—and to stand fiercely opposed to them is okay. But even in those moments, we should still be compelled and blanketed by God's big love.

1. When have you recently felt compelled to extend God's big love to someone else?

2. When have you recently experienced God's big love through someone else?

In order to love other people wholeheartedly, we need to experience God's unconditional love in our lives. Paul prayed over the church in Ephesus—that they might fully experience the love found in Christ. This prayer can be echoed for people even today.

3. Read **Ephesians 3:16–19**. How does being rooted and grounded in God's big love on a daily basis affect your attitude and response toward other people?

The book of Jude was written to faithful Christians to warn them about false teachers. This tiny book tucked near the end of the New Testament is full of good instruction. Jude offered four commands to faithful Christians.

4. Read **Jude 20, 21**. What four commands did Jude give his audience? What does keeping yourself in the love of God look like for you?

5. What tends to cause you to wander from God's love?

6. In the chart below, match the passage with the word that best describes the love we're meant to have for one another.

Scripture		Description	
Deuteronomy 10:19		Fervent	
Matthew 22:39		Proof of commitment to Christ	
John 13:35		Impartial	
Romans 12:9		Abounding	
1 Peter 1:22		Without hypocrisy	
1 Thessalonians 3:12		Unselfish	

7. Reflecting on the list above, which description would you like to see in your own expressions of love?

8. Read **John 15:13** and **1 Corinthians 13**. Whom do you sense God is calling you to love big? What's stopping you from reaching out to this person and extending God's love?

God
equips us to love
others by saturating us with
His love. As we receive His
love, we're empowered to
love others big.

Digging Deeper

Read **Romans 5:8** and **Ephesians 2:4, 5**. What are some clear ways God demonstrated His love for humanity? What are three specific ways God demonstrated His love for you? How can you share that love with someone else today?

Bonus Activity

Memorize **Jeremiah 31:3**. Copy the verse on a sticky note or on the mirrors in your house with a dry erase marker. Each time you walk by, be reminded of the big love God has for you. Look for opportunities to share the message of this verse with others this week.

A time of war,
And a time of peace.

Ecclesiastes 3:8

A Time to Trust

Faith in God's Faithfulness

A man once traveled to work alongside Mother Teresa at her Home for the Dying in Calcutta, India. He hoped to develop a clear answer to how he should spend the remaining years of his life.

The first morning he had the privilege of meeting Mother Teresa. She asked him matter-of-factly, "What can I do for you?"

The man asked for prayer.

Mother Teresa pressed him. "What do you want me to pray for?" she asked.

The man paused and thought how best to express what he longed for. Only one word came to mind: clarity. He made the request of Mother Teresa.

She refused. "No, I will not do that."

The man was baffled. Why wouldn't this beloved saint offer this simple prayer request?

"Clarity is the last thing you are clinging to and must let go of," Mother Teresa explained.

The man protested. After all, Mother Teresa always seemed to have the clarity that he longed for.

"I have never had clarity," Mother Teresa answered. "What I have always had is trust. So I will pray that you trust God."[1]

No matter what situation we're facing, God asks us to trust Him. At times, we'll find ourselves facing conflict in our life, workplace, family, and world. Other times, we'll find ourselves in seasons of peace when we can reflect and reassess. Ecclesiastes reminds us, "[There's] a time of war, and a time of peace" (3:8). Whatever season we're in, we can seek God for clarity. We can ask God to give us the best course of action for the future. But sometimes, God doesn't answer us specifically. Such moments give us the opportunity to grow in trust for God and enjoy the journey we're on—knowing that He is with us.

"I have never had clarity," Mother Teresa answered. "What I have always had is trust."

1. When you're facing the unknown, do you tend to ask for greater clarity or greater trust? Explain.

The journey of following God requires trust. This is demonstrated time and time again throughout the Scriptures. We're reminded of the importance of trust—no matter what season we're in—in Hebrews 11. The unknown author of Hebrews writes that faith is being sure of the invisible—just like God in creation. He made what was unseen, seen.

2. Read **Hebrews 11:1–3**. What can God accomplish when we trust in Him?

3. What is one area of your life where God has asked you to trust Him in the past? How did God show Himself faithful in that area?

Hebrews 11, often referred to as the "Hall of Faith," lists men and women throughout Israel's history who placed their trust in God and were rewarded by God's faithfulness. The author repeats the phrase "by faith," driving the point that faith is central to the believer's life.

4. Read **Hebrews 11:4–7**. What is the most difficult aspect of trusting in God for you?

Abraham followed God, even though he didn't know where he was going, and trusted God to fulfill promises that were impossible to obtain apart from divine intervention. Abraham lived during a time when many gods were worshiped. When God came to Abraham and asked him to leave behind everything he knew, Abraham displayed great faith and obeyed. Though the fullness of the promises God made to Abraham in Genesis 12:1–3 didn't come to fruition in his lifetime, Abraham still chose to trust God.

5. Read **Hebrews 11:8–19**. What aspect of Abraham's faith journey would have been the most difficult for you? Explain.

The author of Hebrews lists great leaders, influential prophets, and unlikely characters who all have one thing in common: they placed their trust in God. Two specific women are named in the Hall of Faith. Sarah and Rahab were unlikely women who displayed great faith in their lives. Portions of their stories can be found in Genesis 12, 16–18 and Joshua 2 and 6.

6. Read **Hebrews 11:20–40**. What do those who choose to trust God obtain through their faith? What do they not obtain (hint: vv. 39, 40)?

7. What does **Hebrews 11** reveal to you about the importance of trust in your faith journey?

8. Reflect on all of the seasons mentioned by Solomon in **Ecclesiastes 3:1–8**. Which season is God asking you to trust Him with right now? What's stopping you from fully trusting Him with this season of life?

The
journey of faith
calls us to trust God no
matter what seasons of
life we're facing.

Digging Deeper

Read **Genesis 12:1–5**. How did God ask Abraham to trust Him? What did God promise Abraham He would provide? What aspect of God's request do you think required the most trust from Abraham? What area of your life requires you to trust God the most? How have you grown by trusting God in this area?

Bonus Activity

Gather together the participants of your Bible study or a bunch of friends and have a painting party. Choose to use finger paint, watercolors, or acrylics, and gather the supplies needed. Spend time in fellowship as you create a painting that reminds you of the seasons of life. Design an artistic piece displaying Ecclesiastes 3:1–8 in words, shapes, scenes, or images. Use your imagination and create a masterpiece to remind you that God is faithful during all seasons of life.

Leader's Guide

Chapter 1: A Time for Everything
Spring and Summer, Winter and Fall

Focus: Every season of life provides an opportunity to learn something more about God. Though we don't always get to choose our season of life, we can always choose to call out to God and worship Him in the midst.

1. Encourage participants to have fun discussing their favorite season. Do they enjoy the watermelon and backyard BBQs of summer? Or the Christmas lights and Advent season of winter? Use this question as an icebreaker to get to know the participants in the group.

2. As participants are breaking the ice with the first question, continue the discussion. Seasons of nature can be reflective of real life seasons. Fall and winter are sometimes seasons of loss, whereas spring is a season of new life. Encourage participants to find the season that best represents their current stage in life.

3. Answers will vary. Everything Solomon describes is by God's hand, meaning that He is in control. God doesn't call us to literally hate or kill; instead, the author reminds us that no matter what, God is still in control. The point of Ecclesiastes is to describe that nothing can be understood or purposeful without God.

4. Acts 16:25 describes Paul and Silas praying and singing hymns to God, even after being beaten and thrown into prison for serving Him. Despite their circumstances, Paul and Silas praised the Lord.

5. When we face rough situations, blaming God may be easier than worshiping Him. Through the story in Acts 16, we can be encouraged and challenged to praise God no matter what the situation.

6. God sent an earthquake to release Paul and Silas from prison. God listened to their faithful prayers and set them free from the situation.

7. During difficult times the bad things happening can sometimes consume us, and we forget to look for how God is working through the circumstance. We may not always expect to see God revealing Himself during troublesome times.

8. Encourage participants to consider how God may be revealing Himself to them in their current situations. During a tough financial time, He may be revealing Himself as the Provider. During a physical malady, God may be revealing Himself as the Healer or Comforter. During a time of joy and gratitude, God may be pushing them to be thankful always and pour His goodness into the lives of others. Spend time in prayer asking God to continue revealing Himself to each participant in a new way.

Digging Deeper

If God asked us those questions, we might be humbled and awestruck by God's magnificence and sovereignty. Knowing that God created everything and holds everything together gives us comfort. Our small difficulties or the rough seasons of our lives shrink in comparison to God's greatness.

Chapter 2: A Time for New Beginnings
Called to Something Fresh

Focus: God is in the business of making all things new. Sometimes God uses the community that we're in to do something new to share the love of Christ with others. Other times God wants to do something new within. Both can make us more Christlike.

1. Answers will vary. Allow this question to be an icebreaker for the meeting time. Have fun laughing and interacting with one another as everyone discusses what new things excite them and those that make the group cringe.

2. We would love to hear the innovative ideas from your ministry! Email them to info@margaretfeinberg.com or post them on Margaret Feinberg's Facebook or Pinterest page. If someone can't think of something they have been a part of, spend time brainstorming needs that can be met and creative ways to do so. Many times these new experiences can bring out personality traits such as leaders, followers, designers, encouragers, listeners, inviters, and many more. Every role and gifting is needed when participating in ministry.

3. God desired to free the Israelites from oppression in Egypt through Moses. He desired to give them a good and spacious land, flowing with milk and honey.

4. Answers

Scripture	Moses' Concern	God's Response
Exodus 3:11, 12	Who am I?	I will certainly be with you.
Exodus 3:13–15	What is Your name?	I AM WHO I AM or I AM sent you.
Exodus 4:1–9	What if they don't believe me?	Here are three signs as proof to them.
Exodus 4:10–12	I'm not a good speaker.	I created you and will teach you what to say.
Exodus 4:13–17	Just send someone else.	I will send your brother Aaron with you.

Often when God calls us to do things, we may find ourselves making similar excuses.

5. Encourage participants to share about people they know or have heard of who are sharing Christ's love to others. Spend time praying for them and their ministries. Consider making them a meal or writing them a note of encouragement this week.

6. The Holy Spirit may be nudging participants to step out and try something new to share Jesus' love. Like Moses, we may be tempted to let excuses and other responsibilities pile up. Spend time praying that God will be clear and lay what He wants each participant to do on his or her heart.

7. God is doing new work when we choose to give our lives to Christ. The old is gone and the new is here.

8. Answers will vary. While some people may still wrestle with holding on to the new and letting go of the old self, others may not have noticed a large change. Remember some in the group may not have made the decision to give their lives to Christ yet. Spend time in prayer for each participant to fully understand and grasp what being a new creation in Christ means.

Digging Deeper

The writer of this poem described a difficult time in Israelite history, making his words even more personal. Often when faced with trials and hardships, doubting God's lovingkindness is easy. This passage may reflect some of your laments to God. Verses 22, 23 describe that despite the afflictions in life, God is still faithful.

Chapter 3: A Time for Necessary Endings
Leaving Behind the Familiar

Focus: Sometimes we hold on to things that aren't God's best for us and we face a necessary ending. But when we let go, we can begin to lay hold of the new beginning God has for us.

1. This may include breaking off relationships or ties with a friend, or moving to a new city, or changing churches. Often our necessary endings happen in everyday life and don't have to be monumental changes. While at first the ending may seem difficult or sad, when looked at in light of the new beginning God has in store, we can find comfort.

2. Often our necessary endings take a toll on our body, mind, and soul. Encourage the group to share how that has been true in their lives.

3. Jesus asked Levi to follow Him and Levi rose and left everything behind to follow Jesus. Often following Jesus means giving up things that make us comfortable, but following Jesus is never something to regret. The new beginning Jesus offers is one free from guilt and condemnation and brings new life and grace.

4. Often when we hold tight to things in our lives, we have to let them go in order to fully discover what God has for us. Jesus calls us to take up our cross and follow Him. We must fully lose our lives before we can find them.

5. Answers will vary.

6. The sacrifice that we can experience is Christ's sacrifice for us. Perhaps some in the group will have experienced this for the first time within the past year.

7. Encourage participants to share a time when they gave their time, money, or resources as a meaningful sacrifice to someone else. While this may not be something everyone wants to discuss, gently encourage those who want to share to do so. Hearing another's story may bring ideas and opportunities for others to grasp what sacrificing for others means.

8. Often selfishness and fear can hold us back from laying hold of the necessary endings God is calling us toward. Spend time praying for God to reveal to each participant what areas of his or her life He is calling to an end and to find comfort in the promise of new beginnings.

Digging Deeper

Abram and Lot needed to part ways because the land could not support them both. Abram responded with civility by providing a solution to the problem: Lot could choose his part of land, and Abram the other. Abram was rewarded when God promised to give him all the land he could see. In the necessary ending of Abram and Lot sharing land, God promised Abram a new beginning. The land that was promised to Abram later became the land of Israel—the home of God's people.

Chapter 4: A Time to Transition
The Importance of Change

Focus: Change isn't easy for most people. But rest assured that whenever you face a time of transition God is with you. He longs to see you flourish and to bring you to a more fruitful life in Him.

1. Change can be difficult because transition may pull us out of our comfort zones. When we get used to a routine or city we live in, change can bring anxiety or frustration. While some of us may be invigorated by new opportunities and adventures, others may feel burdened and uncomfortable.

2. Joseph's father seemed to be extremely thankful for the opportunity to live in Pharaoh's land. He blessed Pharaoh and was able to settle in the best part of the land.

3. The descendants multiplied greatly in the land.

4. Often in times of change or transition, we feel God's blessing in our lives. Whether through the provision of a new job, financial stability, or a great church and relationships to invest in, God often blesses us when we follow His lead and put down roots in new things.

5. The new pharaoh (a title like the word "king") came into power. This pharaoh was suspicious of how numerous the Israelites were, so he began to oppress the people—making them slaves. In order to escape the injustice and murder of Hebrew babies, the Israelites needed to leave Egypt.

6. Just like we discussed earlier, there is a time for necessary endings and new beginnings. In the same way, our necessary endings may lead to a time of uprooting and transition. Navigating through transition can depend on how we handle change. No matter what changes in our lives, understanding that God remains constant is important. He is always with us.

7. During certain seasons of our lives, we may find one description more meaningful than the other. Those in transition may find both verses comforting.

8. Encourage the participants to share areas of their lives that are in transition. Use this as a time to get to know one another better and pray for each other as we all experience times of transition.

Digging Deeper

Jesus met His followers as they were leaving town after Jesus' death. The disciples didn't recognize Him at first. Luke described how Jesus was the Messiah who was prophesized about for centuries before. Often uneasiness in times of transition can be comforted through prayer and reading Scripture. Scripture depicts many stories of people undergoing transitional periods—times for planting and uprooting—throughout the centuries.

Chapter 5: A Time to Heal
Hope for the Wounded

Focus: God longs to bring healing and restoration in every area of our lives. We can entrust ourselves to God as our Healer.

1. Often the physical wounds are easier to heal than internal wounds. Encourage the group to share which is true for them. Remind participants that God is the Healer of all wounds—visible and invisible. He desires to bring healing to each of His children.

2. God is a God who heals the brokenhearted and binds up the wounds of His people. Encourage participants to share times when God has stepped in and healed emotions—whether those times involved relationship wounds, emotional abuse, or moments of depression.

3. God asked His people to listen carefully to the voice of the Lord and do what was right in His eyes. He asked them to pay attention to His commands and keep His decrees.

4. Answers

Scripture	Healing Available to Us
Psalm 41:4	For our sins
Jeremiah 3:22	As a cure for backsliding
Luke 4:18	To free the captives and the oppressed, and heal the blind

5. The seasons of life bring about different needs for healing. For some, healing of physical maladies is needed while others may require healing in relationships or for past wounds.

6. Answers will vary, but the descriptions in Revelation 22 are hope-filled and encouraging.

7. This passage describes that God desires to give us a new heart and spirit.

8. Set the tone and intimacy level of the group by sharing first. When everyone has finished sharing, spend time lifting up those requests in prayer. Be consistent in praying for these things as often as possible.

Digging Deeper

In rest, we find time to set aside for restoration and renewal. When we cram our schedules and don't allow time for healing, we can delay the healing process. But when we set aside time for rest, we begin to feel renewed and restored from the inside out. This week, consider setting aside a portion of time for rest—a chance for God to offer you healing and restoration.

Chapter 6: A Time to Reassess
Breaking Down and Building Up

Focus: Knowing what season we're in—a time to downsize or a time to expand—requires us to seek God. The best way to reassess our lives is to prayerfully submit everything to God and live wide-eyed to the ways He answers.

1. Some participants may be more willing to reassess certain areas of their lives above others. Often we are the most willing to reevaluate the areas we don't hold onto very tightly—like a frustrating job or a time commitment we aren't thrilled about.

2. Often, we may find it difficult to reassess things we find most comfortable. If it's working in our minds, why would we reassess? We can find this to be true in our relationships or in a well-paying job.

3. God's plans, thoughts, and timing rarely line up with our own. However, when we step back, we realize that God's plans, thoughts, and timing are so much greater and better than ours. We may have seen this to be true when we tried to take something into our own hands instead of trusting God.

4. God may have asked us to join a small group or make a big move in jobs or across town. While God's request may not have made sense at the time, we can often find comfort in the outcome of being faithful and surrendering to God.

5. Gideon reassessed his military force by allowing those who were fearful to go back. The passage in Deuteronomy describes how those who were afraid could return home. There may be times when God has asked us to scale back in the amount of time, money, or resources we give out. While God's request may not have made sense at the time, it may have provided us renewal and rest.

6. God revealed to Gideon that He would give the Midianites into his hands. Gideon didn't have anything to worry about because God was on his side. Often we can be encouraged through Scripture, prayer, and encouragement from godly friends.

7. Gideon and his three hundred men defeated a large army—without even fighting. They followed God's instructions and God delivered their enemies into their hands.

8. Spend time sharing the instances in which God is revealing how His ways are better than ours. Spend a few minutes in prayer asking God to continue pushing each participant to surrender everything to His perfect and pleasing will.

Digging Deeper

James 1:5 promises that God gives wisdom generously. Psalm 18:30 promises that God's way and His Word are perfect. Because God's will is perfect and He gives wisdom generously, we can find comfort in surrendering all areas of our lives to God.

Chapter 7: A Time to Remain Faithful
Continuing Through Hardship

Focus: Whether our current season of life is marked by hardship and pain or great joy and celebration, we can remain faithful knowing that God remains with us.

1. Encourage participants to share moments in their lives when they have wept, laughed, mourned, and danced. Use this time as a chance to get to know your group better.

2. Throughout all seasons of life, God is with us! No matter if we are crying, laughing, mourning, or dancing, God goes before us and is with us. Share moments in your life when God has revealed Himself to you in these situations.

3. Zacharias and Elizabeth trusted that God was in charge—no matter what happened. While remaining faithful during difficult situations can be frustrating, we can be encouraged that God has a plan for us because He loves us.

4. Answers will vary as we don't know exactly what Zacharias and Elizabeth felt, but we can assume the couple was sad, ashamed, and disappointed when they found out they were infertile. When the angel met them, they probably felt shock, awe, and fear. Finally, when their child was born, they probably felt elation and gratitude, and they may have even danced.

5. During periods of waiting on God, we can feel frustrated, sad, and disappointed. We may assume that what we desire to happen may never happen and decide to take things into our hands.

6. Answers will vary. The psalmist, David, expressed emotions of praise, thanksgiving, desperation, anger, rejoicing, security, dismay, and joy.

7. Encourage the participants to share a moment in their lives when they experienced God stepping in and turning their wailing into dancing. God reaches into the desperate and hopeless moments in life and answers prayers—like Elizabeth's and Zacharias's.

8. As participants share intimate moments in their lives when they cry out to God, spend time praying for each individual. Ask that God may surround them with comfort and peace and turn their sadness into joy.

Digging Deeper

As Jesus read from this passage, He basically said, "This scripture defines Me. I am the Messiah you've been waiting for." We can find comfort in this message because Jesus cares for those hurting and in mourning. Jesus comes to bring healing and gladness.

Chapter 8: A Time for Fruitfulness and Replenishment

Gathering and Scattering

Focus: Being fruitful as followers of Jesus requires seasons of productivity and seasons of replenishment. We can trust that God is at work no matter what season we're in.

1. In our lives we go through seasons when God asks us to produce, and others when God asks us to dig our roots deeper into Him. Perhaps God is calling us to a time of investing in a ministry, or maybe He is asking us to spend time being nourished by others and His Word.

2. Answers will depend on personality types. Maybe we're the type who enjoys pouring into others. Or maybe we would rather read and meditate on God's Word and be poured into.

3. Spend time sharing the group's beautiful artwork. Consider bringing colored pencils, glitter, crayons, and construction paper and setting up a craft time.

4. Those who meditate and delight themselves in God's law are fruitful. On the other hand, those who hang out with sinners, mockers, and scoffers are like chaff (the empty shells)—fruitless.

5. Martha served wholeheartedly. She prepared and was hospitable to her guests. She was fruitful in her approach to serving Jesus.

6. Mary sat at Jesus' feet and gleaned from His teaching. She took time to become replenished and root herself in Jesus.

7. Often, taking the opposite method can grow and stretch our faith. While it may not seem comfortable or natural at first, God calls us to seasons of fruitfulness and to seasons of replenishing.

8. Spend time in prayer asking God to reveal areas in the lives of participants where time is needed to serve and give to others, and other areas where time is needed to slow down and replenish. Encourage participants to set aside an hour during the next week to serve and give to others and another hour to slow down and rest. Next time you meet, share with your group how those hours encouraged and filled you up.

Digging Deeper

In the end, God brings growth. No matter what our role, God works through us and in us. Even in times when growth and fruitfulness seem impossible, God takes care of it.

Chapter 9: A Time for Resolutions

Following Through

Focus: Whenever we resolve to become more Christlike, we can seek God through prayer. He will strengthen us, extend grace to us, and provide the courage to make any necessary changes in our lives as we seek Him.

1. Often our resolutions revolve around these areas: we want to lose weight, read our Bible more, or spend more time with our families. Consider how your resolutions reflect a God-led goal to make you more like Jesus.

2. As the introduction shared, participants are better able to accomplish their goals when they share them with others. Spend time sharing one resolution that each participant wants to accomplish. Encourage participants in their goals and check back often to see how they are going.

3. By answering these questions, we are better able to reflect on our goal and even better able to accomplish it. Encourage your group to spend time answering these questions and refocusing their goals.

4. Answers

   Psalm 66:20: God does not reject prayers.

   Isaiah 65:24: God hears and answers prayers before they are spoken.

   Matthew 21:22: If we believe, we will receive whatever we pray for.

   Romans 8:26: The Spirit intercedes on our behalf.

   James 5:16: When we pray for each other and confess our sins, we may be healed. A righteous person's prayers are powerful and effective.

5. Answers

   1 Chronicles 16:11: We are called to seek God's strength.

   Psalm 18:32–34: God offers His strength to strengthen us.

   Isaiah 40:28–31: He gives power to the weak.

   1 Corinthians 10:13: God gives us strength to endure temptation.

   Philippians 4:13: We can do all things through Christ who strengthens us.

6. Answers

   Romans 5:21: Grace reigns through righteousness to eternal life through Jesus Christ.

   2 Corinthians 12:9: God's grace is sufficient for us.

   Hebrews 4:16: God's throne is full of grace—so that He can pour it out to us in our time of need.

   James 4:6: God gives us more grace.

   2 Peter 1:2: We gain grace in the knowledge of God and Jesus.

7. Answers

   Deuteronomy 31:6: By giving us courage, God goes with us and will never leave us nor forsake us.

   Joshua 1:3–9: God is with us even in difficult and new times. He encourages us to be strong and have courage.

   Psalm 27:1: Why should we be afraid when God is our strength?

   Romans 8:15: The Spirit of God doesn't bring us fear, but makes us His sons. We have nothing to fear.

   2 Timothy 1:7: God's Spirit doesn't make us fearful, but gives us power, love, and a sound mind.

8. God desires that we fall more in love with Him and become more and more like Jesus along the way. Spend time in prayer lifting up each participant's resolution. Ask God to surround the group with His strength, grace, and courage as each person journeys to become more Christlike.

Digging Deeper

Zacchaeus promised to give half his possessions to the poor and pay back, four times over, those he had cheated. Instead of spending his life swindling others, Zacchaeus wanted to be more like Jesus. Jesus approached the small man and invited Himself to his house. This sparked a change in Zacchaeus—the Messiah wanted to hang out with him, even though he wasn't the most honest man.

Chapter 10: A Time for Silence and Speaking
The Value of Knowing the Difference

Focus: Sometimes God calls us to speak up. Sometimes God calls us to remain silent. To discern the difference, we can seek God through prayer.

1. Esther risked her life by approaching the king's throne, but did so in order to save the lives of thousands. In our lives, when we find ourselves in a difficult situation, we can be encouraged that God is still at work.

2. If Esther had revealed her nationality from the get-go, she probably wouldn't have become queen. But when the time came, Esther spoke up and revealed who she was in order to save thousands of lives. Just like in the life of Esther, God gives us positions of influence where we are to remain silent or speak up to do amazing things for Him.

3. Answers may vary. Remind participants of God's grace and compassion.

4. Answers may vary. Remind participants of God's grace and compassion.

5. Answers

Psalm 34:13: We should keep our tongue from evil and our lips from speaking deceit.

Proverbs 11:9: The hypocrite can destroy his neighbor with his mouth.

Proverbs 11:12, 13: Those with understanding hold their peace. Faithful people keep secrets.

James 1:26: Those who do not bridle their tongues deceive their own hearts.

1 Peter 3:10: They should keep their tongues from evil and keep their lips from speaking deceit.

6. Answers

John 3:11: We are to testify what we have seen and what we know.

Romans 1:16: We are not to be ashamed of the gospel.

Colossians 3:16: Let the word of Christ dwell in us richly as we teach one another.

1 Peter 3:15, 16: We should always be ready to give a defense to everyone who asks us to give a reason for our hope.

Hebrews 13:15: May our lips openly give thanks to His name.

7. We can turn to God for discernment through prayer.

8. There may be situations or conversations where God is nudging us to remain silent. There may be other areas where God is calling us to speak up—whether on Christ's behalf or to be a voice for the voiceless. Spend time in prayer asking God to reveal areas in our lives where we need to hold our tongues or speak up.

Digging Deeper

James compared the tongue to a bit on a horse, the rudder of a ship, and a spark of a fire—small things that control something greater. Our speech holds a position of great power with the ability to hurt or praise someone.

Through just words, we can build or break down relationships. Spend time praying that God will give you the wisdom and discernment as to how to use your speech to glorify Him—through relationships, conversations at work, or moments of praising God. There is a time for speaking and a time to remain silent—ask that God reveal these two situations to you this week.

Chapter 11: A Time for Love
Reaching Out to Others

Focus: God equips us to love others by saturating us with His love. As we receive His love, we're empowered to love others big.

1. Providing free babysitting to overwhelmed parents or sending a note of encouragement to a neighbor or friend are times when we can show God's big love to someone else.

2. Perhaps a friend or co-worker extended love to a participant by taking her out to coffee or surprising her with an encouraging phone call.

3. Being rooted and grounded in God's love defines the foundation of our every action, thought, and word.

4. Jude instructed the faithful Christians to build themselves up on their most holy faith, pray in the Holy Spirit, keep themselves in God's love, and look for Jesus' mercy to bring eternal life. We are encouraged to keep in God's love. For some, this may include reading and meditating on God's Word and remaining constant in prayer.

5. Answers will vary; for some, wandering from God's love can happen when other things in our lives consume us. When we seek our meaning and definition in the world, we can forget how deeply we are loved by Christ.

6. Answers

Scripture	Description
Deuteronomy 10:19	Impartial
Matthew 22:39	Unselfish
John 13:35	Proof of commitment to Christ
Romans 12:9	Without hypocrisy
1 Peter 1:22	Fervent
1 Thessalonians 3:12	Abounding

7. The descriptions of love from the above question are qualities we would all want to describe the ways we love others. Some adjectives may resonate more with different participants. Consider other biblical descriptions of love like 1 Corinthians 13.

8. God calls us to lay down our lives for our friends in unselfish love. Encourage participants to consider the people in their lives whom God is laying on their hearts to love. Challenge participants to step out of their comfort zones and love big on those individuals this week.

Digging Deeper

God loved us so much that He sent His son to die so that we can be reconciled to Him. God has shown His love to us in His mercy, forgiveness, provision, sacrifice, creation, and redemption. God offers big love each and every day. Spend time brainstorming ideas how the group can show that same love to someone else today.

Chapter 12: A Time to Trust
Faith in God's Faithfulness

Focus: The journey of faith calls us to trust God no matter what seasons of life we're facing.

1. Often our prayers may be for clarity—seeking clear vision as to what path we should take or decision should be made. Other times, we pray for trust—the ability to trust God even in the unknown. Both prayers are opportunities to give our control over to God.

2. God can accomplish the impossible when we trust in Him. The possibilities are endless.

3. God may have asked you to trust Him with finances, a big move, or a job offer. When we place those areas in God's hands, we can see how He is faithful to us. Spend a few minutes praising God for His faithfulness in your life.

4. The most difficult aspect in trusting God may be trusting Him in the unknown. Rather than give a situation over to God, we may want to take matters into our own hands.

5. For some, going into an unknown land and leaving behind what is comfortable may be the most difficult. For others, trusting God during times of infertility may be the most difficult. For others, sacrificing their only son may be impossible to consider—even though God asked Abraham to do so.

6. None of those listed received what had been promised in their lifetime. Instead, in faith, they trusted God to work through them to accomplish a greater goal—the coming of Jesus Christ.

7. As we place our trust in God, He is able to use us for His greater purpose. When we don't see the fruit of our labor, we can have faith that God is bringing everything together for His purpose and His will.

8. God may be asking each participant to trust Him in multiple areas of life. Spend time in prayer asking God to reveal areas to give over to Him in trust.

Digging Deeper

God asked Abraham to trust Him and leave his country. Abraham probably needed to trust that God would provide and protect him and his family. The areas where we need to trust God the most are sometimes financial or relational.

Notes

Chapter 3

1. J. Lee Grady, *Fearless Daughters of the Bible* (Grand Rapids: Chosen Books, 2012), 60.

Chapter 6

1. Lois Tverberg, *Walking in the Dust of Rabbi Jesus: How the Jewish Words of Jesus Can Change Your Life* (Grand Rapids: Zondervan, 2012), 15, 16.

Chapter 8

1. Tracey R. Rich, "Tu B'Shevat," Judaism 101, http://www.jewfaq.org/holiday 8.htm.

Chapter 9

1. Richard Wiseman, "New Year's Resolution Experiment," Quirkology: The Curious Science of Everyday Lives, http://quirkology.com/UK/Experiment_ resolution.shtml.

Chapter 11

1. George H. Guthrie, *The NIV Application Commentary* (Grand Rapids: Zondervan, 1998), 351.

Chapter 12

1. Brennan Manning, *Ruthless Trust: The Ragamuffin's Path to God* (New York: HarperCollins, 2002), 5.

About the Author

A popular speaker at churches and leading conferences such as Catalyst and Thrive, Margaret Feinberg was recently named one of the 30 Emerging Voices who will help lead the church in the next decade by *Charisma* magazine. She has written more than two dozen books and Bible studies, including the critically acclaimed *The Organic God, The Sacred Echo, Scouting the Divine,* and their corresponding DVD Bible studies. She is known for her relational teaching style and inviting people to discover the relevance of God and His Word in a modern world.

Margaret and her books have been covered by national media, including CNN, the Associated Press, *Los Angeles Times,* Dallas Morning News, *Washington Post, Chicago Tribune,* and many others. She currently lives in Colorado with her 6'8" husband, Leif, and superpup, Hershey. Go ahead, become her friend on Facebook, follow her on Twitter @mafeinberg, add her on Google+, or check out her website at www.margaretfeinberg.com.